For my sons.
—D. P.

For land stewards past,
present, and future.
—D. P. & M. M.

Library of Congress Cataloging-in-Publication Data available.

ISBN 978-1-7972-1450-4

Manufactured in China.

MIX
Paper | Supporting
responsible forestry
FSC™ C136333

Design by Jill Turney.
Typeset in Myriad and More Pro.
The illustrations in this book were rendered digitally.

10 9 8 7 6 5 4 3 2 1

Chronicle books and gifts are available at special quantity
discounts to corporations, professional associations, literacy
programs, and other organizations. For details and discount
information, please contact our premiums department at
corporatesales@chroniclebooks.com or at 1-800-759-0190.

Chronicle Books LLC
680 Second Street
San Francisco, California 94107

Chronicle Books—we see things differently. Become part of
our community at www.chroniclekids.com.

THEY HOLD THE LINE

Wildfires, Wildlands, and the Firefighters Who Brave Them

by Dan Paley

illustrated by Molly Mendoza

chronicle books · san francisco

Perched on a tall tower at the edge of the wilderness, someone waits and watches. She is a fire lookout. She waits and watches for fire.

A lookout is the eyes above the forest. She sees a hundred miles in every direction. She is watching as a dry thunderstorm rolls over the timbered horizon.

A lookout's job is as lonely as it is important, except for those who bring their dogs. During fire season, they live alone in a cabin or atop a lookout tower, keeping an eye out for smoke, tracking the weather, and communicating fire behavior to crews engaged on the ground.

Lightning strikes. Tree bark sparks and smolders. In the distance, a finger of white smoke pokes through the canopy. The lookout calculates the location of the fire and alerts dispatch. *"Smoke report!"*

Two-Way Radio

Azimuth: The horizontal bearing of a point measured clockwise from true north; used by lookouts to determine the location of a fire

Binoculars

Canopy: The crowns of the tallest vegetation in an area

Dispatch Center: A center that mobilizes resources to a fire incident

Osborne Firefinder: A topographic map encircled by a rotating metal ring equipped with a sighting device called an alidade; used by lookouts to determine an azimuth

Belt Weather Kit: A kit of tools used to measure wind speed, wind direction, humidity, and dew point

FIRE WEATHER INFORMATION NOTEBOOK

Lightning is the most common natural cause of wildfire in dry regions such as the American West. But the most common cause of all wildfire is human activity—unattended campfires, arson, downed power lines, or even sparks from locomotive wheels on railway tracks.

From a small plane circling overhead, parachuters swing and soar. They are smokejumpers. They swing and soar to the site of the fire. Smokejumpers provide the initial attack. They fly over rugged terrain by plane and chute.

Cargo Drop: A drop of equipment or supplies from an aircraft to a designated place called a drop zone

Jumpsuit: A suit worn by smokejumpers

Heat, oxygen, and fuel are the three things a fire can't live without. Firefighters know that they can contain a fire by removing any one of those components. The easiest to remove is fuel, often by digging something called a fireline, or handline, which looks like a hiking trail. Firefighters remove trees and shrubs along this strip of land, then light small fires with drip torches, burning up fuel to slow the wildfire. This technique is called backfiring.

Jump Spot: A landing area for smokejumpers

Fuel: Any combustible material; in a wildfire, this includes logs, trees, dead sticks, branches, twigs, grass, fallen leaves, and pine needles

They fight fire without water. They use hand tools—Pulaskis, Rhinos, McLeods, chain saws—to cut away trees, shrubs, and roots, so fire can't crawl across the vegetation. They set a fireline to limit the fire's spread until other resources arrive. "*Timber!*"

Drip Torch: A handheld device for igniting fires by dripping flaming liquid fuel; used by firefighters to consume fuel inside a fireline

Fireline/Handline: A strip of land cleared of fuel, designed to contain a fire

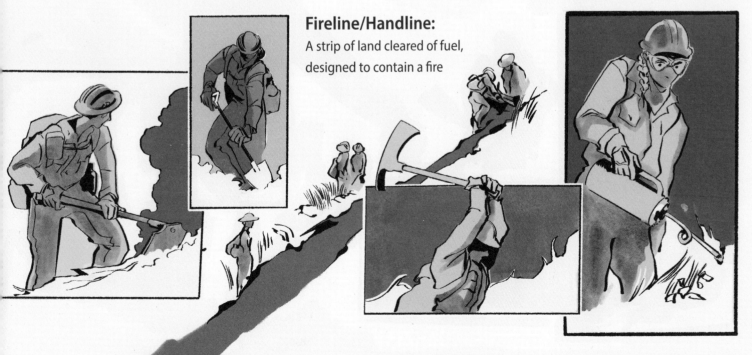

Swamper: A crew member who carries equipment and helps clear away the things fallers cut down

Handcrew: An 18- to 20-person crew that uses hand tools to construct firelines

Stationed at a base deep in the forest, a handcrew plans and prepares. It is an elite hotshot handcrew. It plans and prepares for fire. Crew members are called hotshots because they work on the hottest part of a fire.

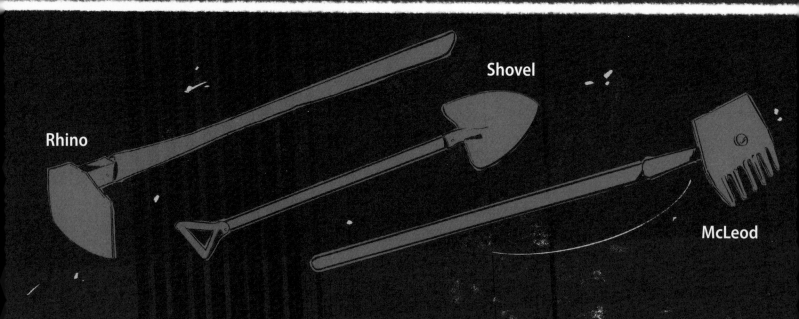

Rhino

Shovel

McLeod

Faller/Sawyer: A crew member who uses a chain saw to bring down trees and other large vegetation

Burn Boss: A crew member who directs prescribed fire operations

When not fighting fire, firefighters spend a couple of hours each day lifting weights, hiking with packs, or running. This prepares them to carry gear and to reach fires many miles away.

They do not slide down poles or ride in shiny red trucks. They are hikers and campers—part lumberjack, part mountain goat. They are stewards of the land.

Pulaski

Chain Saw

Combi-tool

The radio crackles. The crew receives its assignment from dispatch. Crew members grab their gear and roll out. They begin the long hike through the forest.

They march alongside the angry inferno. They trudge through ash up to their knees. The hotter the flames, the smarter they work. They dare not confront the fire head-on. They maintain a safe distance. They reinforce the fireline.

Trench: A deep fireline dug into a slope to prevent burning logs and pine cones from rolling downhill and spreading a fire

Anchor Point: A natural barrier, such as a road, from which to construct a fireline; natural barriers and firelines combine to form a control line

Topography plays an important role in fire behavior. Fire burns uphill faster than downhill because, as smoke and heat rise, fuel above is preheated and dried. Firefighters must be aware of their surroundings and have well-planned escape routes, especially in hilly terrain.

A crew member stops to watch a doe and her fawn skirt the fire's edge. The deer pause to look back on their burning home, then leap off in search of safety.

Some animals are very good at avoiding fire. Large mammals such as deer and elk flee; ground animals tunnel below fast-moving surface-level fires; birds fly away. Slow-moving and young reptiles, the eggs and nestlings of ground birds, and tree-bound species such as koalas are more likely to die in large, fast-moving blazes. Life and death often depend on how fast and far the fire spreads.

While fires can be deadly to many species, most of the effect on animals is realized in the months *after* a fire, as they contend with food shortages and habitat loss. Some leave for good in search of food and protection. But most return within hours after a fire. Many species of birds are *attracted* to burn areas because hunting is easier—there are fewer places for prey to hide!

At a makeshift camp in a high school parking lot, people assemble and support. They are a base crew. They assemble and support the long fight. All around them—in their noses and hair and clothes—is the thick smell of fire.

They cook meals. They set up tents and showers. They do laundry. They provide a place for firefighters to rest and plan their next moves. The firefighters are thankful for hot meals and much-needed showers and some rest before dawn.

On small fires, firefighters sleep in tents or nearby cabins. But for large fires that can stretch for weeks, bases are set up to support efforts. Firefighters endure long days, and during fire season, they can spend months away from their families. A base provides a home away from home, a place where tired firefighters can rest and regroup. The volunteers who work there remind firefighters that they are supported by a community and that they have a community to protect.

Back on the front line, a sudden gust of wind flares up a wall of fire. Embers rocket through the air. The hotshots stand down and retreat to safety. They hear the fire roar like an oncoming freight train and feel the sting of heat on their necks. Someone is hurt. A helitack crew rappels down ropes to extract the injured firefighter. *"Fall back!"*

Blowup: A sudden spread of fire that overwhelms efforts to control it

Advancing Fire/Forward Fire/ Running Fire: A part of a wildfire that spreads rapidly and with high intensity, often aided by wind

The fire has jumped across the line. The firefighters have lost containment. They double their efforts, day and night, to regain control. The hours stretch into days and the days into weeks under the hazy murk of the smoke-filled sky.

Snag: A dead tree that is still standing and can fall during a fire

Helitack Crew: A crew of firefighters specially trained in the use of helicopters

Escape Route: A preplanned route firefighters take to move to a safety zone

Evacuation Harness: Equipment used for short-haul rescue evacuation by helicopter

Safety Zone: An area cleared of flammable materials and used for escape in the event that a fireline is overrun

Medevac: The evacuation of an injured firefighter to a hospital and the medical care provided while in transit

Firefighting is extremely dangerous. High winds can quickly change the direction of a fire. Firefighters battle heat exhaustion, smoke inhalation, and dehydration. In addition to the fire, they must look out for dead trees and branches that can fall without notice. Snakes, yellow jacket nests, rolling rocks and logs, and sharp tools add to the hazard of an inferno.

On the outskirts of a nearby town, people hurry to evacuate. They are in the path of the approaching fire.

Wildfire moves fast. People in harm's way must be prepared to evacuate at a moment's notice.

Wildlands burn and regenerate in a natural process of ecological renewal—human-made communities do not. Pollutants from ash and burned materials seep through soil and land in streams and reservoirs, killing fish and contaminating drinking water. This can make a burned area unsafe for human habitation.

Some planned ahead. Others are awakened in the middle of the night. They escape with only their pets and the clothes on their backs. They say goodbye to their homes, not sure what will be left when they return.

The firefighters call for reinforcements. A drone opens an eye in the sky. An airtanker swoops over the treetops and paints the forest red.

Both helicopters and airtankers drop water on fires. Airtankers also drop red fire retardant on the fuel that surrounds a fire to strengthen the fireline.

Airtanker: An aircraft used to deliver water or fire retardant

Bambi Bucket: A bucket carried below a helicopter; used to scoop and transport water

Fire Retardant: A substance or chemical agent that reduces the flammability of fuel

Dozer: A vehicle with a front-mounted blade used for digging down to mineral soil; short for bulldozer

Booster Reel: A reel for the booster hose, mounted on a fire engine

Fire engines and water tenders from other states arrive at the scene. They pass cars twisted by heat and charred houses with only the chimneys left standing. They lay hose and pump water up the hillside. A dozer carves its way through the brush. Together, they reset the line.

Booster Pump: An intermediary pump used to pump water beyond the capacity of the first pump

Booster Hose: The most common type of hose used on wildland fire engine booster reels

Containment: The status of firefighting efforts measured as the percentage of the fire that is surrounded by the control line

Mop-Up: The extinguishing of burning material after a fire, to make an area safe

Bulldozers multiply the efforts of line building, quickly digging wide trenches to stop fire from spreading. Fire engine crews use a complex system of hoses, pumps, and valves called a hose lay. They connect the water source to the site of the fire. They manage water pressure to ensure a powerful delivery of water.

Finally, the fire weakens. The firefighters begin the long, messy mop-up of the simmering fire. All around them is the sizzle and snap of pinesap. At last, the fire is contained.

Meandering through the forest, a crew is slogging back to base. The crew members are exhausted and ashen, tired and aching. They are slogging but smiling, because the fire is out.

Wildland firefighters work 16-hour days, 14 days in a row, with 1-hour rest periods for every 2 hours of work. This is called a roll. In peak season, they might work 18 to 24 hours per day, often straight through the night. They also travel across the United States, and to and from as far away as Australia, to assist on large fires.

When at last a fire is contained, they will rest if they can, but they're always ready for the next fire call.

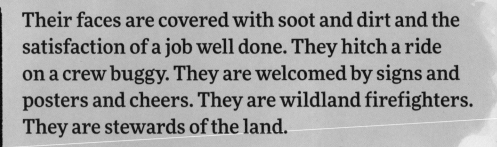

Their faces are covered with soot and dirt and the satisfaction of a job well done. They hitch a ride on a crew buggy. They are welcomed by signs and posters and cheers. They are wildland firefighters. They are stewards of the land.

The fire is out because they held the line.

Fire Ecology

Few natural disasters are as fearsome as wildfire. The small spark of a few dry pine needles can quickly grow into a megafire that burns hundreds of thousands of acres, threatening farms and towns. Yet wildfire is critical to the health of many ecosystems. In fact, in North America, some 80 percent of plants and trees evolved along with fire. Pyriscence, for example, is an adaptation in plants that requires fire or smoke to trigger the release of seeds. Fires open gaps in forest canopies that let in sunlight, helping the seedlings of giant sequoia compete with other species. In chaparral communities, the leaves of some plants are coated in flammable oils that *encourage* fire. Imagine that!

So why can such an important natural feature of the landscape also be so dangerous? To answer that question, we must understand that not all fires are disasters—that there is a difference between harmful fire and beneficial fire. Yes, the presence of fire where it shouldn't be can be catastrophic, but the absence of fire where it *should* be can create even bigger, delayed disasters. We must also understand how human interference with the natural course of fire in the landscape sets up a dangerous balancing act that wildland firefighters are all too often called on to negotiate.

History of Fire Management

For thousands of years, Indigenous peoples across North America and the world stewarded the landscape by burning it with light, prescribed fires. Prescribed burning thins the buildup of fuel in a forest and promotes ecological health. But as early as 1793, Spanish colonists in California saw fire as a threat to their cattle's pastureland and banned Indigenous burning. In 1850, California outlawed burning under the Act for the Government and Protection of Indians. The US Forest Service was established in 1905 to protect the timber supplies in newly dedicated national forests. A final blow came with the Great Fire of 1910—a series of fires in Montana and Idaho that burned three million acres in just two days, killing more than 85 people and sending smoke as far away as New York. As a result, wildfire was further characterized as an enemy threat to the United States' timber industry. The US Forest Service waged war on fire, with the goal of removing it from the landscape. Over the next 50 years, a kind of obsession took over. Some 5,000 lookout towers were erected to spot and extinguish fire as quickly as possible. In 1935, the US Forest Service issued the "10:00 a.m. policy," which decreed that a fire must be suppressed by 10:00 a.m. the day after it was spotted. Adding to these efforts, elite hotshot crews were established—first in Southern California in the 1940s, in the Cleveland

and Angeles National Forests, and then across the West. Smokejumpers also began operating in the 1940s in Idaho. Suddenly, both naturally occurring and human-introduced fire were removed from the landscape.

Fire ecologists and wildland managers now understand what all this suppression has done to the landscape. Ecosystems that depend on wildfire have been robbed of the natural cycle of burning and renewal. Dry fuel that would normally burn off with frequent small fires has built up over decades. In addition, the burning of fossil fuels to power cars and industry has led to a changing climate, with warming temperatures and drier conditions driving bigger and hotter fires. Our landscape has become a hot, dry, dead tinderbox waiting to ignite the megafires we see today. Even so, more and more communities are being built in flammable wildland. This puts firefighters in the risky position of trying to protect homes and lives. As fires have become larger and more frequent, firefighters' death tolls have grown as well. According to the National Wildfire Coordinating Group, between 1910 and 1996, 699 firefighters died while battling blazes. In just the past 30 years, nearly 500 have died.

A New Approach

In the 1960s and 1970s, public and private agencies began reintroducing fire to the landscape through prescribed burns. And by 1978, based on that success, the US Forest Service finally moved on from its strategy of total suppression. Today, fire managers are learning to live with fire. In some places, they thin forests manually by removing trees. In others, they work, sometimes with Indigenous leaders, to restore fire to its natural place in the landscape through prescribed burns. They fight fire with fire! Remember: This is extremely dangerous and should only be done by professionals. They are also working to develop more fire-resilient communities, using fireproof building materials and clearing brush away from structures. Finally, they are choosing to let more fires burn rather than always putting firefighters in harm's way. Sure, when fire threatens a community like the one in this story, it does seem like firefighters are waging all-out war against an enemy invader. But the opposite is just as true—firefighters also protect wildlands from human interference. Indeed, most of their work goes unseen by the news footage of large, bad fires. Increasingly, modern fire management is moving away from a losing battle against fire and toward more stewardship of the land in harmony with it. After all, fire isn't going away. It's up to us to decide what kinds of fires we have. In that sense, we are all land stewards.

Who Are Firefighters?

In addition to being brave and physically fit, firefighters must understand ecology, land conservation, and weather patterns. They don't just put out fire and protect things from burning—they are caretakers of the land, preserving it for future generations.

Firefighters come from many backgrounds. Some start as park rangers. Some smokejumpers have a military background. Many study science in school, care about conservation, and hope to undo the damage done to the environment.

Some of the most elite hotshot crews are Native Americans. The Bureau of Indian Affairs operates seven hotshot crews that contribute to national efforts. All seven crews—Chief Mountain, Fort Apache, Geronimo, Golden Eagles, Navajo, Warm Springs, and Zuni—are located on Native American reservations.

An unjust source of firefighters is, in some states, prison. The policy dates to World War II, when firefighting forces were depleted by the war. In California, incarcerated people who meet certain requirements can apply to become firefighters in exchange for less time in prison. The California Department of Corrections and Rehabilitation operates fire camps across the state where incarcerated crews live and work. But despite going through the same training and braving the same hot, dirty, and dangerous conditions as other firefighters, they earn only a few dollars per day. What's worse, once released from prison, most are not allowed to work as firefighters because of their criminal records. Not until 2021 did California pass a law allowing formerly incarcerated people to work as firefighters.

Protective Gear and Supplies

- Helmet
- Headlamp
- Hearing protection
- Goggles
- Shroud
- Yellow flame-resistant shirt
- Gloves
- Green flame-resistant pants
- Drip torch
- Boots

Safety First!

In 1957, a task force commissioned by US Forest Service chief Richard E. McArdle studied tragedies that occurred over the previous 20 years. The result was the 10 Standard Firefighting Orders. The US Forest Service later added 18 Watch Out Situations. They are known as the 10s and 18s. Firefighters keep these lists with them to review as part of their daily safety check.

10 STANDARD FIREFIGHTING ORDERS

❶ Keep informed on fire weather conditions and forecasts.

❷ Know what your fire is doing at all times.

❸ Base all actions on current and expected behavior of the fire.

❹ Identify escape routes and safety zones, and make them known.

❺ Post lookouts when there is possible danger.

❻ Be alert. Keep calm. Think clearly. Act decisively.

❼ Maintain prompt communications with your forces, your supervisor, and adjoining forces.

❽ Give clear instructions, and be sure they are understood.

❾ Maintain control of your forces at all times.

❿ Fight fire aggressively, having provided for safety first.

18 WATCH OUT SITUATIONS

 **1** Fire not scouted and sized up.

 **2** In country not seen in daylight.

 **3** Safety zones and escape routes not identified.

 **4** Unfamiliar with weather and local factors influencing fire behavior.

 **5** Uninformed on strategy, tactics, and hazards.

 **6** Instructions and assignments not clear.

 **7** No communication link with crew members or supervisor.

 **8** Constructing line without safe anchor point.

 **9** Building fireline downhill with fire below.

 **10** Attempting frontal assault on fire.

 **11** Unburned fuel between you and fire.

 **12** Cannot see main fire; not in contact with someone who can.

 **13** On a hillside where rolling material can ignite fuel below.

 **14** Weather becoming hotter and drier.

 **15** Wind increases and/or changes direction.

 **16** Getting frequent spot fires across line.

 **17** Terrain and fuels make escape to safety zones difficult.

18 Taking a nap near fireline.

Source: *Incident Response Pocket Guide* (National Wildfire Coordinating Group, 2022).
See the National Interagency Fire Center for more information.

Author's Note

The idea for this book began with a question. In August 2018, I stood on the front stoop of my home in Southern California with my three boys. Together, we watched the flames of the Holy Fire dance on a distant ridge in the Cleveland National Forest. Fire was a fact of life for all Californians that year—in our communities, on our television screens. Earlier that summer, the Ferguson Fire had burned 100,000 acres, and the Mendocino Complex Fire had burned 450,000 more. Later that year, the Camp Fire would burn 150,000 acres, killing 85 people and destroying the towns of Paradise, Concow, and Magalia. All told, the 2018 fire season was, at the time, the deadliest and most destructive ever recorded in California.

Not two years later, those records fell, as storms fired thousands of bolts of lightning onto the drought-stricken landscape, sparking hundreds of small fires that combined to form massive ones. The August Complex Fire became the largest in California's recorded history, a gigafire that burned more than one million acres across seven counties. The Castle Fire, also in 2020, and the KNP Complex Fire, in 2021, scorched Sequoia National Park and Forest, killing approximately 10,000 giant sequoia trees—entire old-growth groves that had lived with less intense fire for thousands of years. While working on this book through such destructive years, I often recalled the question my sons asked on that August night, which seemed simple enough: *Who protects us from those fires?* This book is an answer to that complicated question.

Illustrator's Note

While working on the illustrations for *They Hold the Line*, I found myself drawing constantly from the memory of the colors of recent wildfires. Over most of my ten years living in Portland, Oregon, I remember a handful of gray-skied morning commutes to work, peppered by white ash. After biking, my shirt would be stained black where that soot had mingled with my sweat. I remember a red moon at night and commenting on it to friends, blissfully ignorant of what would soon be the reality lapping at the edges of the porch.

In 2020, I remember a noxious yellow, being unable to breathe, and the pink of the air filters in the masks many of us wore. I remember the photos of nearby neighborhoods, closer to the fires outside Salem, and how they'd been painted a neon red at dawn, blanketed by a quiet, eerie menace. I remember the suffocating bruises over maps of the Pacific Northwest on news feeds, muddy purple to indicate that we had the worst air quality in the world at that very moment; the green notification lights of people checking in; the orange-red of the carbon monoxide detector going off; a buzzing black-blue in the middle of the night as we talked about where we would go or what we would do. I learned quickly in those weeks and continue to learn more every year as the threat of wildfire becomes the norm. I appreciate blue skies even more now than I think I ever have. I also appreciate the land stewards who fight to keep these fires at bay and understand that it is a fight that will take all of us to persevere.